11 05

Muhammad Ali

*Muhammad Ali (known then as Cassius Clay) composes
a poem predicting that he will knock out his opponent,
Doug Jones, in the sixth round of their upcoming fight in
March 1963. Ali, one of the greatest boxers in history,
also became a symbol in the fight for black civil rights.*

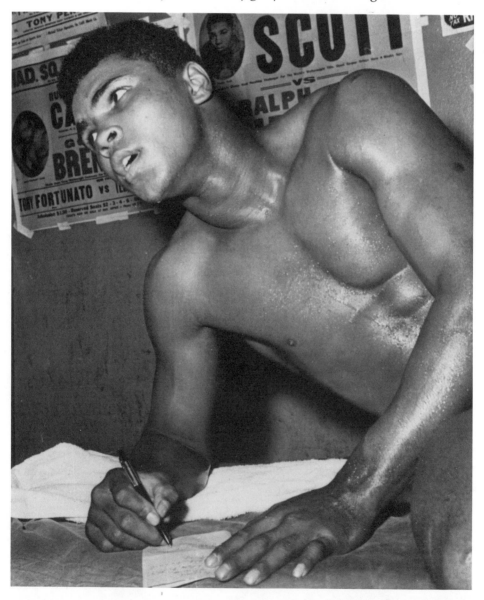

JUNIOR ■ WORLD ■ BIOGRAPHIES

Muhammad Ali

NORMAN MACHT

CHELSEA JUNIORS

a division of CHELSEA HOUSE PUBLISHERS

Chelsea House Publishers

EDITORIAL DIRECTOR   Richard Rennert
EXECUTIVE MANAGING EDITOR   Karyn Gullen Browne
EXECUTIVE EDITOR   Sean Dolan
COPY CHIEF   Robin James
PICTURE EDITOR   Adrian G. Allen
ART DIRECTOR   Robert Mitchell
MANUFACTURING DIRECTOR   Gerald Levine
SYSTEMS MANAGER   Lindsey Ottman
PRODUCTION COORDINATOR   Marie Claire Cebrián-Ume

JUNIOR WORLD BIOGRAPHIES

SENIOR EDITOR   Kathy Kuhtz

Staff for MUHAMMAD ALI
ASSOCIATE EDITOR   Terrance Dolan
EDITORIAL ASSISTANT   Mary B. Sisson
SERIES DESIGN   Marjorie Zaum
PICTURE RESEARCHER   Sandy Jones
COVER ILLUSTRATION   Alan J. Nahigian

The Chelsea House World Wide Web site address is
http://www.chelseahouse.com

3 5 7 9 8 6 4 2

Library of Congress Cataloging-in-Publication Data
Macht, Norman L.
     Muhammad Ali/Norman L. Macht.
       p. cm.—(Junior world biographies)
     Includes bibliographical references and index.
Summary: A biography of the controversial boxer, Muhammad Ali.
ISBN 0-7910-1760-5
       0-7910-1966-7 (pbk.)
1. Ali, Muhammad, 1942– —Juvenile literature. 2. Boxers (Sports)—United
States—Biography—Juvenile literature. [1. Ali, Muhammad, 1942– . 2.
Boxers (Sports) 3. Afro-Americans—Biography.] I. Title. II. Series.
GV1132.A44M33 1993   92-28925
796.8'3'092—dc20   CIP
[B]   AC

Contents

Ali throws a right cross to the head of Leon Spinks during their rematch in New Orleans in September 1978. Spinks had captured the heavyweight title from Ali eight months earlier.

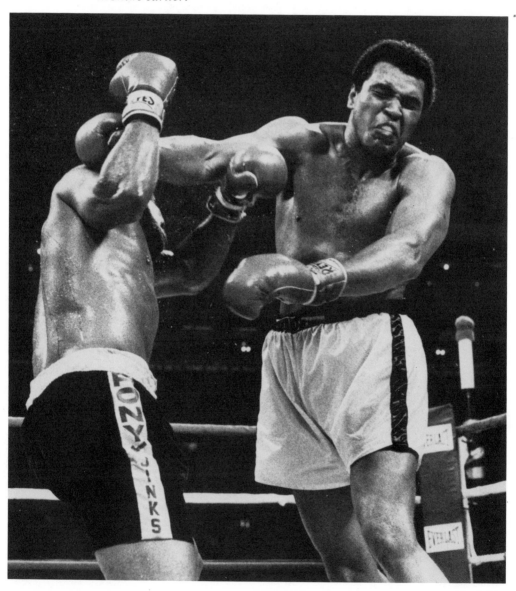

1

"The Greatest"

On September 15, 1978, 63,532 fans packed into the New Orleans Superdome. They were there to see the battle for the heavyweight championship of the world. It was the largest indoor crowd ever to see a prizefight. Across America, millions of people gathered around televisions to watch the fight. The ABC television network was showing the *bout*. The TV broadcast of the fight enjoyed the second largest viewing audience ever. Around the world, in countries where the fight could not be seen on TV, millions of people huddled around radios to listen to the action.

A boxing ring had been set up in the gigantic Superdome. In the ring, two fighters stood in their corners waiting for the bell that would start the first round. In one corner was the champion, 24-year-old Leon Spinks. Eight months earlier, not many people had even heard of Leon Spinks. He was a former U.S. Marine from the ghettos of St. Louis, Missouri. Before the night of February 15, 1978, Spinks's greatest boxing achievement had been at the 1976 Summer Olympics, where he captured a gold medal in the light-heavyweight division. After that, he had turned to professional boxing as a heavyweight. During his short professional career, he had fought only eight times. He had won seven of his eight fights; one was declared a draw. Up until his eighth contest, he was just another young, hopeful, unknown fighter. But then came the night in February 1978 in Las Vegas. On that night, Spinks had become heavyweight champion by defeating the man whom many considered the greatest prizefighter of all time—Muhammad Ali.

Now, eight months later, it was Ali who stood across the ring from Spinks in the Superdome, determined to regain his title. And it was Ali who was responsible for the huge crowd and the worldwide interest in the bout. Ali was the most famous athlete of the second half of the 20th century. He had exploded onto the boxing scene in the early 1960s. There had never been a prizefighter like Muhammad Ali. During the prime of his career, his boxing talents had seemed almost supernatural. "I am the greatest!" he told anyone who would listen, and a lot of people believed him.

Back then, Ali had been an artist of the ring. His hands were as fast as lightning. They were so fast that he once knocked out an opponent with a punch nobody saw until they looked at the slow-motion replays. His legs were strong and swift. His movements were agile and graceful. He glided around his opponents like a dancer. His reflexes were so quick that he was often impossible to hit. He could "float like a butterfly and sting like a bee," in the words of one of his supporters. When he did receive a heavy blow—and he had been hit by some of the hardest punchers in heavyweight history—he was able to absorb the punch and come back fighting. And he used *strategy* in the ring like no other fighter before him.

But Muhammad Ali was much more than a boxer or an athlete-hero. His influence reached far beyond the ring. The force of his personality—his *charisma*—had extended into politics, religion, and race relations. The strength of his beliefs in these issues and his courage in standing up for his beliefs against great odds had made him an international figure. To millions of blacks, and other *minorities* and oppressed peoples in the United States and around the world, Muhammad Ali was a symbol of power and courage.

Now, all that seemed to be part of a distant past. Ali, at 36 years old, was no longer the prince of the boxing ring. He had lost his title to somebody that no one had ever heard of. During the first fight with Spinks, in February, Ali had been plodding and slow, unable to defend himself from the swarming attack of the younger man. He had seemed like an aging fighter whose time had come and gone. After the loss to Spinks, many of Ali's friends, trainers, and even doctors had urged him to retire. The magic was gone; time had finally caught up with Ali. He could be seriously hurt in another fight. But Ali was not listening. He only wanted one thing—a rematch with Leon Spinks. He wanted his title back. Despite the pounding he had taken from Spinks, he began training for the rematch the next day at dawn.

Muhammad Ali's long career had seen many great moments. His second fight with Leon Spinks was to be the last of them. Ali no longer had the speed or reflexes of his younger days. He could no longer dance circles around his opponents or leave them dazed with blinding combinations of punches. But what Ali did still have was his intelligence in the ring and his experience as a fighter. During the second fight with Spinks, he used every trick and technique he knew. He smothered the young fighter's onslaught, tying up Spinks's arms when he was close. He hugged Spinks and leaned his full weight on him for long

Spinks unsuccessfully tries to trap Ali in a corner as Ali escapes to his left while blocking Spinks's punches. Ali was awarded a 15-round decision in his rematch with Spinks, becoming the first fighter to win the heavyweight championship three times.

periods, relaxing and saving his own strength while Spinks used up his energy by struggling to free himself. He kept Spinks off-balance with jabs and occasionally punished him with a hard right. Often, a simple step to the left or right by Ali would leave the lunging Spinks tangled in the ropes.

During the early rounds, Spinks was frustrated by Ali's tactics. By the middle of the fight, Spinks was deeply confused. By the time the last rounds arrived, he was tired and badly demoralized. Now Ali opened fire with lefts and rights, jabs and uppercuts. When the final bell rang after 15 rounds, the referee raised Ali's hand in the air. The huge crowd in the Superdome stood and roared. People smiled and cheered in front of their television sets across America. Celebrations broke out around the world, especially in African and Islamic countries. Things were as they should be: Muhammad Ali was once again heavyweight champion of the world.

Cassius Clay at age 12 in 1954, the year he first began boxing in a gym in Louisville, Kentucky. By the age of 16, Clay was one of the best young fighters in Kentucky.

2
The
Louisville Lip

Muhammad Ali's original name was Cassius Marcellus Clay, Jr. He was born on January 17, 1942, in Louisville, Kentucky. His father was a sign painter, and his mother, Odessa Grady Clay, worked as a cook and housecleaner. The parents of Cassius Clay, Sr., were not slaves, nor were their parents. But it is likely that some of Cassius's distant ancestors were slaves. One of Odessa Grady Clay's grandparents was the son of a white man and a slave named Dinah.

Although the Clays had little money and lived in one of the poor, black sections of town, there was always enough to eat, even if it was simple food. There were seldom new clothes to wear, but the boys' mother always managed to dress them up nicely for Baptist church on Sundays. Cassius had a happy early childhood. He was surrounded by relatives. For many years, four generations of Clays lived on the same street. Cassius especially liked his aunts Coretta and Eva. All of Cassius's family members remember that young Cassius loved to talk.

Louisville, Kentucky, like most of the American South at that time, was a *segregated* city. Blacks were mostly poor, and they lived in the run-down parts of town. As a boy, Cassius Clay was aware of the racist conditions in his hometown, and he resented them. But the true nature of racial hatred in America did not hit home for Cassius until he heard about the murder of Emmett Till. Emmett Till was a 14-year-old black boy who was visiting an uncle in Mississippi. Three white men who believed Till had insulted a white woman beat him, shot him, and threw his corpse into a river. The murder of Emmett Till outraged blacks across the South, especially when the three white men went free. Young Cassius was deeply affected by the incident. "I felt," he remembered later, "the need to do something for my people."

During the autumn before Emmett Till was murdered, when Cassius was 12, his father gave him a brand new bicycle for Christmas. It was a handsome bike, with red lights, chrome trim, and whitewall tires. Cassius was proud of it. One day Cassius and a friend were riding around town on their bicyles. They stopped at a bazaar and went inside to eat cotton candy. When they came out, Cassius's bike was gone.

Frantically, Cassius ran about the neighborhood. He began to cry. Someone told him he could find Joe Martin, an off duty policeman, in a nearby gym. Cassius opened the door and looked inside. The room was filled with boys of all sizes, black and white. Cassius stopped crying and his eyes widened. He watched and listened to the sights and sounds of a boxing gym. Some boys pounded punching bags. Others shadowboxed silently. Still others *sparred* inside a ring, exchanging punches. Cassius Clay had discovered his world.

At the age of 12, Cassius became a regular at Joe Martin's gym. He was a tall, gangly, 112-pound kid. Martin began teaching him the *fundamentals* of the science of boxing. At first, there seemed to be nothing special about Cassius except for his determination. During sparring matches, he was often bloodied or knocked on his rear end by more experienced fighters. But Cassius was never daunted. "I realized it was almost impossible to discourage him," remembers Martin. "He was easily the hardest worker of any kid I ever taught."

Cassius trained day and night, sometimes six days a week. When he was not in school, he was training. Within a year, his natural talents had begun to show. He had remarkably quick hands and nimble feet. He had the reflexes of a cat. And he had great stamina. He was gaining weight and

18

strength. His skinny frame was beginning to fill out. He began fighting amateur bouts. In 1955, he entered the Golden Gloves tournament but lost to an older fighter named Kent Green. He returned to the gym, worked harder, and continued fighting on the amateur level.

During the next five years, Cassius fought more than 100 amateur bouts. His brilliance as a boxer began to shine. By 1960, he had won six state Golden Glove tournaments, two national Golden Glove tournaments, and two national AAU (Amateur Athletic Union) titles. That year, at age 18, he qualified for the U.S. boxing team and flew to Rome, Italy, to represent his country

Clay (right) exchanges left jabs with Jimmy Jones on his way to victory during a Golden Gloves championship fight at Chicago Stadium in March 1960.

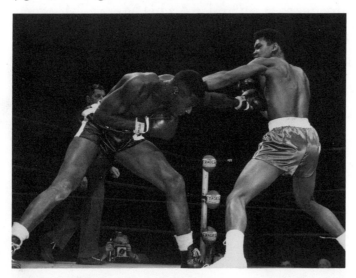

in the Summer Olympics. Fighting as a light-heavyweight at 178 pounds, he won the gold medal, rallying in the last round of the final bout to beat a tough, experienced Polish fighter.

Clay returned to Louisville for a parade in his honor. He was proud of his Olympic achievement. He wore his red, white, and blue USA team jacket wherever he went. But Clay had other things on his mind: It was time for him to become a professional prizefighter. A group of wealthy Kentucky businessmen agreed to manage his career. What he needed most now was a professional trainer. Without a good trainer in his corner, even the best of fighters is at a disadvantage. As Clay would find out, a trainer can mean the difference between victory and disaster in the ring.

Clay's managers decided to send him to California to train under Archie Moore. Moore, a former light-heavyweight champion, was 47 years old. He had started boxing in the 1930s and since then had fought almost 200 fights. Moore had battled some of the great fighters of the 1940s and

1950s, including the unstoppable heavyweight champion Rocky Marciano. (Like just about everyone who fought Marciano, however, Moore ended up unconscious.)

Clay's managers felt that Moore would be the perfect trainer for their young heavyweight. (Clay was now big enough to fight as a heavyweight, weighing about 190 pounds.) But Clay and Moore did not see eye to eye. Moore disapproved of Clay's fighting style. Moore also thought Clay was a spoiled loudmouth. "The boy," Moore said, "needed a spanking." Clay did not intend to accept a spanking from anyone, and he returned to Louisville.

The search for a trainer continued. In December 1960, Angelo Dundee signed a contract to train Clay. Dundee was (and still is) known as one of the best trainers in boxing. He recognized Clay's unique gifts and did nothing to try and change them. Instead, he worked with Clay to perfect his style, to build his stamina, and to teach Clay how to think in the ring and use his talents to the utmost. Dundee would remain with Clay throughout his career. As far as boxing was concerned, nobody would be more important to Clay over the years than Dundee.

Clay began fighting other pro heavyweights on a regular basis. He beat them one after another. Some fights he won by decision. Others he won by knockout. Dundee and Clay's managers began putting Clay in the ring with tougher, more experienced fighters. Clay beat them. All of these early opponents emerged from their fights with Clay with a single thought—they had never seen anything like him in a boxing ring. Sportswriters and fight fans began to take notice of the tall, lean heavyweight with the fast hands and swift feet.

When Clay was not fighting, he was talking. He talked about one thing and one thing only—Cassius Clay. He talked constantly, and he talked to anyone who would listen. He talked to sportswriters, fight fans, radio talk-show hosts, other fighters in the ring, even people on the street. He would walk up to strangers, introduce himself, and inform them that he was going to be the next heavyweight champion of the world. Reporters nicknamed him The Louisville Lip.

One night in his dressing room before a fight, Clay predicted that he would knock out his opponent, a fighter named Willie Bessemer, in the seventh round. To the astonishment of everyone but Clay, Bessemer was knocked out in the seventh. Clay began making predictions before every fight. "They'll all fall in the round I call," he boasted. Fight after fight, his predictions proved correct. Sometimes, he would make his prediction in the form of a little poem. Before he met the aging Archie Moore in a 1962 bout, he recited: "When you come to the fight, don't block the aisle and don't block the door. You will all go home after round four." Archie Moore, who felt that the brash young Clay needed a spanking, got a spanking himself that night. Clay knocked him out in round four. Clay continued to fight, and he continued to win. He also continued to talk. But now he began talking about fighting Sonny Liston.

Clay avoids the powerful left hook of Sonny Liston during their first fight in February 1964. Most people believed that the fearsome Liston would destroy the young, inexperienced Clay.

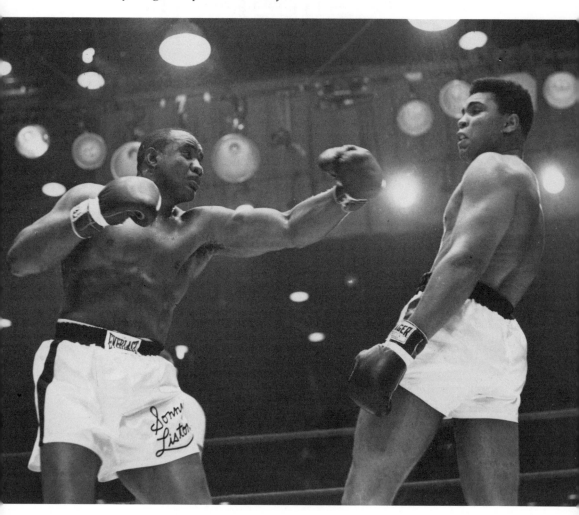

CHAPTER

3
"I Shook Up
the World!"

Sonny Liston was a dangerous man. In his time, he was the most feared fighter in the history of heavyweight boxing. He was a hulking, heavily muscled gladiator with an ugly temper, an ugly scowl, and an ugly past. He had been in and out of prison as a young man for such crimes as armed robbery and beating up a policeman. He learned to box in a Missouri penitentiary. Once he got out of prison, he began fighting as an amateur and then as a pro.

Boxing kept Liston out of trouble with the law. But Liston spelled trouble for his opponents. As he worked his way through the heavyweight ranks, he quickly earned a reputation as a destroyer. He had tremendous punching power in both hands. His fights usually ended with his opponents crumpled in the corner of the ring. But Liston was no clumsy slugger. He understood boxing and boxing techniques, which made him all the more dangerous. And Liston gave the impression that he was an angry person. Often, his mere entrance into the ring was enough to unnerve his opponents. He would stare at them as if they were annoying insects that he meant to crush at the first opportunity.

By 1960, Liston had earned a shot at the heavyweight title. Except for a loss by a close decision back in 1954, he had wrecked every heavyweight in his path. But now (understandably) nobody wanted to fight him. The heavyweight champion at the time was a tough, smart fighter, Floyd Patterson. Patterson managed to avoid Liston for two years. But as heavyweight champion, it was his duty to fight the number-one contender—Sonny Liston.

In 1962, Patterson finally signed a contract to fight Liston. They met in the ring in Chicago on September 25, 1962. It took Liston exactly two minutes and six seconds of the first round to hammer Patterson to the floor and claim the heavyweight championship. The huge crowd that watched the fight was stunned into silence by the destructive force of Liston's blows.

Once he had recovered from his first meeting with Liston, an embarrassed Patterson wanted to sign up for a rematch. He fought Liston again in Las Vegas in July 1963. This time, he managed to survive four seconds longer than the first bout before Liston knocked him out. Boxing experts began to use words like "invincible" when they discussed Liston.

When Clay started talking about fighting Sonny Liston, most people just laughed. The Louisville Lip was simply mouthing off again.

When it became clear that Clay was serious, they thought he must be crazy. Cassius Clay taking on Sonny Liston? Liston, the great destroyer? Clay might get killed. Sure, Clay was a gifted, up-and-coming young heavyweight. Yes, he was fast and hard to hit. And it was true, he had yet to lose a fight as a pro. Someday, he might be champ. But Clay was barely 21 years old. He was still young and inexperienced. Look what Liston had done to Patterson, a smart, experienced fighter, a champion, one of the best there was. Fighting the merciless Liston at this stage of his career, everyone agreed, would most likely *end* Clay's career.

But Cassius Clay did not see it that way. He believed he could beat Sonny Liston, whom he called "that big ugly bear." He told anyone who would listen why and how he would beat Liston. "First five rounds, I'll be circling that big ugly bear," Clay told them. "I'll be sticking [jabbing] and moving so fast the cameras won't be able to detect my speed. After he loses his zip in the sixth, I'll start pounding on him. Whop! Whop! Bop!

Seventh round I'll continue shaking him up. Pop! Pop! Eighth round he'll be dazed, he'll be frustrated, he'll be tired and nervous. I'll be on him faster than greased lightning. Whop, whop! Bop, bop! And Cassius becomes the champion of the world! He's too ugly to be the world champ," Clay added. "The world's champ should be pretty like me."

The trouble with Clay's plans was that Sonny Liston did not seem to be interested in fighting him. In Liston's opinion, Cassius Clay was just some kid with a big mouth and a big opinion of himself. Most of the major fight promoters (the people who finance, organize, and advertise boxing matches) agreed. So Clay began his own advertising campaign for a Liston against Clay world championship fight.

Clay talked about Liston constantly. And he began to provoke Liston. He followed the "big ugly bear" all over the place. Then he would taunt Liston, calling him names, challenging him to fight. If Liston went to see a boxing match, Clay would be there, mocking him. When Liston went to Las Vegas to enjoy himself, Clay showed up and made fun of him from across a gambling table. One late night Clay even showed up at Liston's house. Lights went on all over the neighborhood as Clay stood on the front lawn screaming for Liston to come out and fight.

Finally, Liston agreed to fight Clay. He had had enough of the antics of the Louisville Lip. A date and site for the bout was set—February 25, 1964, in Miami. "I predict that he will fall in eight to prove I'm great; and if he wants to go to heaven, I'll send him in seven," Clay predicted before the fight.

"I might hurt that boy bad," was all Liston would say.

When the two fighters entered the ring on the night of February 25, there was only a small crowd in the arena. Clay's antics over the past months had gotten a lot of publicity. But nobody actually thought he could defeat Sonny Liston. Not many people were willing to pay the price of admission to see Liston demolish Clay in a round or two. They figured they could read about it in the papers the next day. Those who did go to the fight, however, witnessed boxing history.

In round one, Clay kept his distance from Liston. He circled and skipped backward and sideways. Liston chased him, but Clay's legs kept him out of harm's way. The chase continued in round two. Liston landed one or two punches, and Clay felt his power. Those punches "shook me," Clay said later. But in round three, Clay unleashed his own attack. His punches were crisp and accurate. And they were startlingly fast—especially his left jab.

Clay's left jab was his primary weapon. It was a straight, sharp punch that shot out like an arrow. Because of his exceptionally long arms, Clay could jab from a safe distance, without fear of being hit himself. Clay used the jab like a marksman. Liston's face began to swell and bleed. The audience, bored up until then, began to sit up and take notice.

In round four, the pattern continued. Clay jabbed and danced away from Liston. Liston chased him, trying to pin him in a corner. Then, disaster struck. Suddenly, Clay's eyes began to burn and water. Something had gotten in his eyes. By the end of the round, Clay could not see. For the first—and last—time in his career, Clay lost his nerve. Returning to his corner at the end of the round, he shouted at Angelo Dundee: "I can't see! My eyes!" How could he go out for round five to face the fearsome Liston now? "Take the gloves off," he told Angelo Dundee. "We're going home."

Dundee pushed Clay down onto his stool and began washing out his eyes. "I can't see," Clay repeated, near panic. "Shut up," Dundee told him. He believed that the solution Liston's trainers were using to stop Liston's cuts from bleeding had gotten into Clay's eyes. When the bell rang for round five, Dundee lifted Clay up and stuffed the mouthpiece into Clay's mouth. Clay still could not see. His eyes were watering heavily and he was blinking constantly. Dundee had one word for Clay: "Run." Then he pushed his fighter into the ring.

Clay ran. He was in constant motion. He backpedaled around the ring. He changed directions unexpectedly. He stayed out of the corners, where Liston might trap him. It was a brilliant retreat. In the meantime, he continued blinking and pawing at his blurry eyes. Liston, sensing Clay was in trouble, chased him. But Clay's legs and reflexes kept him out of the big bear's punching range. By the end of the round, Clay's eyes were clearing. The bell rang; Clay had survived. Sonny Liston, in the meantime, was visibly tired from the chase.

Round six began, and now the hunted had become the hunter. Clay stung Liston's face again and again with cruel left jabs and hard rights. Liston was defenseless. He was too tired; Clay's punches were too fast. When Liston returned to

Pandemonium breaks loose in the ring after Sonny Liston cannot come out for the seventh round of his first fight with Clay. The new heavyweight champion is hugged by cornerman Bundini Brown while trainer Angelo Dundee celebrates.

his corner at the end of the round, his eyes were swollen, his face was badly cut, and his strength was gone.

When the bell rang for round seven, Clay leaped off his stool. But Liston remained seated. The men in Liston's corner signaled to the referee that Liston was finished. He could not answer the bell. Clay jumped high in the air, his arms raised to the sky. Chaos broke loose as people flooded into the ring. Clay had done the impossible. He had beaten Sonny Liston, turning the boxing world upside down. At age 22, Cassius Clay was heavyweight champion of the world. As he was mobbed in the center of the ring, Clay shouted over and over again. "I shook up the world!" he cried. "I shook up the world! You must listen to me! Oh, I shook up the world!"

"I shook up the world!" shouts Cassius Clay following his victory over Liston, one of the most surprising upsets in boxing history.

*Muhammad Ali (formerly known as Cassius Clay),
speaks during a Nation of Islam conference in Chicago in
1968. Seated behind Ali is Nation of Islam leader Elijah
Muhammad. Ali became a member of the Nation of
Islam and took an Islamic name in 1964.*

4

The Prince
in Exile

Cassius Clay had indeed shaken up the boxing world with his defeat of Sonny Liston. But Clay had more "shaking up" to do. On the day after the Liston fight, he announced that he was now a member of the Nation of Islam. The announcement caused more publicity than his remarkable upset of Liston.

Islam is the dominant religion throughout the Middle East, Africa, and parts of Asia. Islam was founded in Arabia in the 7th century by the prophet Muhammad. Members of the Islamic faith, known as Muslims, follow the prophet's teachings as set down in the book known as the Koran. They worship a single god, Allah. The Islamic religion involves much prayer, ritual, self-sacrifice such as fasting, and a strong sense of community among its members. Today, it is the fastest growing religion in the world.

The Nation of Islam, also known as the Black Muslims, was a Black-American Muslim sect. When Clay joined the Black Muslims, they were under the leadership of a man named Elijah Muhammad. The black leader Malcolm X was also a prominent member. The Black Muslims believed in a complete separation of blacks and whites in American society. They preached black pride and black self-reliance.

Cassius Clay joined the Nation of Islam during a period of great racial and social unrest in America. Race relations and the Vietnam War were tearing the nation apart. The *civil rights movement* was gaining momentum under such

Ali signs an autograph for a fan while his friend, Black Muslim minister Malcolm X, waits for him outside a New York City movie theater in 1964. Ali was greatly influenced by the friendship and teachings of Malcolm X.

leaders as Martin Luther King, Jr., and Malcolm X. Blacks across the nation were challenging the racism that had oppressed them since the days of slavery. They were demanding equal rights as American citizens. Many white Americans were unprepared for these changes or simply refused to accept them. There were civil rights marches and riots in the streets. In the South, there were beatings and murders of blacks.

Most whites, and especially those in the U.S. government, saw the Black Muslims as *extremists*. They were considered to be a dangerous element of the civil rights movement. When Cassius Clay joined them, he was criticized harshly by white journalists, white politicians, and many white people around the country. Then, Clay announced that he was changing his name. He would no longer be known as Cassius Clay. Clay was a slave name, he said, given to his black ancestors by their white masters. Now, he was taking an Islamic name—Muhammad Ali. "Changing my name was one of the most important things that happened to me in my life," he said later. "It freed me from the identity given to my family by slavemasters."

In the meantime, Ali was also attending to other things. He fell in love with a beautiful waitress and part-time model, Sonji Roi. They were married on August 14, 1964. (Ali divorced Sonji in 1966.) And Ali was preparing for the rematch against Sonny Liston.

Most sportswriters believed that Ali's first fight with Liston had been a freak occurrence. Liston had not taken Ali seriously enough, they said. He had not trained properly. He had hurt his shoulder early in the fight and could not punch effectively. This time, they were sure, Liston would take care of Ali. This time, Liston would be ready.

But what happened on the night of May 25, 1965, in an arena in Lewiston, Maine, was more shocking than what had occurred in the first meeting between Ali and Liston. Most people—including Liston—believed that Ali would use the same strategy he had used against Liston in their first fight. But when the bell rang for round one, Ali rushed across the ring, straight at Liston. There was a flashing exchange of blows, and then Liston was flat on his back. Ali stood above him, demanding that he get up and fight. But Liston was dazed and confused, and the referee reached the count of 10 before he could struggle to his feet. The fight was over. One minute and 42 seconds had passed since the bell for round one had sounded.

The blow that felled Liston that night became the single most talked-about punch in boxing history—"the phantom punch." Most of the people at the fight that night never saw it. There was talk that the fight was "fixed." Some people believed that Liston was so intimidated by Ali after their first encounter that he took the first chance he got to lie down and stay down. But film replays tell the true story of the phantom punch. Sonny Liston simply ran into a perfect punch. At regular speed, replays show little, for the punch was so fast it appears as a blur. Slow motion, however, reveals a right hand, delivered in a short, straight line from

Ali stands over a stunned Sonny Liston and demands that he get up and fight in the first round of their rematch in May 1965. Liston has just received Ali's famed "phantom punch."

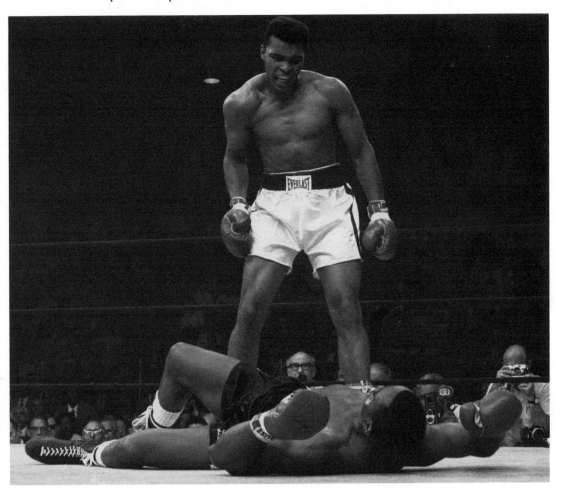

Ali's shoulder, landing perfectly on Liston's chin. After the fight, lying on his dressing room table, Liston was asked if he saw the punch coming. "Yes, but I saw it too late," Liston replied. "Don't let no one tell you that Ali can't punch," he added. Then he requested smelling salts to clear his foggy head.

Ali began looking for new challengers. He found one, but it was an opponent that was bigger and stronger than any he had faced before—the U.S. government. Muhammad Ali had been *drafted* into the U.S. Army.

The Vietnam War was raging in Southeast Asia, and hundreds of thousands of young American men were being drafted. They were sent to Vietnam to fight alongside the South Vietnamese against the *communist* North Vietnamese, who were known as the Vietcong. Ali made it clear from the beginning that he would resist the draft. He had several reasons for doing so. First, it was against the teachings of his new religion. Second, Ali felt that blacks, who were so mistreated in their own country, had no obligation to fight a war being waged by a white government that oppressed its own black citizens. "I'm expected to go overseas to help free people in Vietnam," Ali said, "and at the same time my people here are being brutalized and mistreated." And third, Ali felt that the war itself was wrong. At a press conference in Miami, he expressed the feelings of all the young American men who were also resisting the draft. "Man," Ali said angrily, "I ain't got no quarrel with them Vietcong."

Muhammad Ali was now a villain to many patriotic Americans. Soon, there was not a state in the entire nation that would provide Ali with a license to fight. Ali, determined to continue his career, began fighting in other countries, first in Canada and then in Europe. Ali was now at his peak as a fighter. He was as fast, fluid, and graceful as ever in the ring. But he had also matured physically. His body rippled with muscles. Ferdie Pacheco, Ali's doctor, described the fighter during this period. "If God sat down to create the perfect body for a fighter," Pacheco said, "he'd have created Ali." He could hit with a power that numbed opponents into unconsciousness. Or he could slash them to ribbons with his jab, which he used much like a surgeon uses a scalpel. His superiority to other fighters was so great that he would often toy with them in the ring like a cat toys with a mouse. Sometimes, in the middle of a flurry of punches, he would do the "Ali shuffle," a high-speed shuffling of his feet that looked like a dance routine. Ali's dazzled opponents would look down at this spectacle, and Ali would pop them. Ali left a trail of broken and bloody Europeans in his wake as he fought his way across Europe. It is doubtful that there was ever a heavyweight, before or after Ali, who could have beaten him during this period in his career.

And then, suddenly, at its peak, his career was over. Back in the United States, he was given a final chance to accept the draft. He could serve his term of duty entertaining the U.S. troops in Vietnam. Ali refused. On June 30, 1967, he was put on trial for draft evasion, found guilty, and sentenced to five years in prison. And, perhaps worst of all, he was stripped of his title as heavyweight champion of the world.

Muhammad Ali's career and his life were filled with moments and episodes of courage. There would be many more to come. But in standing up for his beliefs against the power of the U.S. government, Muhammad Ali lost his freedom, his popularity, and the boxing title he had dreamed of and worked so hard for since he was 12 years old. This, perhaps, was the finest and most courageous round Muhammad Ali ever fought.

*Muhammad Ali scores a hard right to the head of Jerry
Quarry during their contest in Atlanta in October 1970.
It was Ali's first fight after being banned from the ring
for three years for refusing to serve in the Vietnam War.*

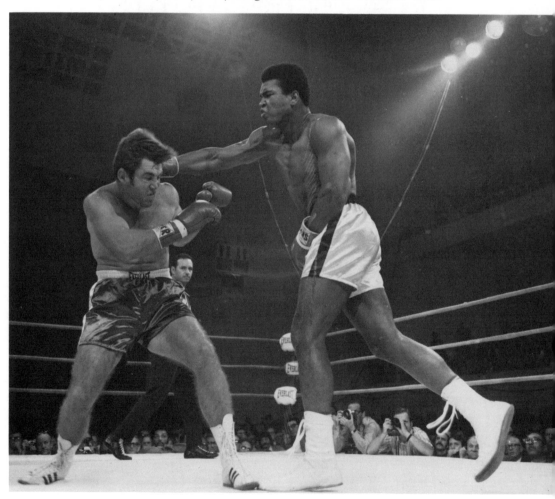

5

The Fight

Ali was permitted to stay out of prison while his lawyers fought his draft-evasion case. But he could not leave the country. He could not fight, which left him no source of income. And he was kept under close watch by the Federal Bureau of Investigation (FBI). But Ali had his faith in Allah, and a new wife, Belinda Boyd Ali. And he had his characteristic optimism. "In the end," Ali said, "I am confident that justice will come my way."

Ali soon learned that he could make some money to support himself and his new wife by doing what he did best (aside from fighting). He talked. He went on a lecture tour of college campuses, where he was a big hit among the many students who opposed the war. He appeared on television and radio talk shows. He expressed his views on the war, on race relations in the United States, on boxing, on his religion, and on anything else he was asked about. And, in the meantime, just as Ali had predicted, justice came his way.

Gradually, public opinion in the United States was turning against the Vietnam War. Thousands of young Americans were sacrificing their lives in a far-off country in a war that the United States apparently could not win. More and more Americans, including some white politicians, were changing their opinion about the treatment of Ali. They were beginning to see that Muhammad Ali was a victim of racial and religious *persecution*. Finally, with the support of a black state senator, Leroy Johnson of Georgia, Ali was granted a license to fight in Atlanta. His opponent would be popular Jerry Quarry, a tough, hard-hitting Irish

American. Three years had passed since Ali's last fight.

Ali's return to the ring took place on October 25, 1970. That night, 80 percent of the audience in the arena was black. It seemed that every important black person in the country was there. The seats were filled with black civil rights leaders, black athletes, black entertainers, black politicians, and any other black citizen of Atlanta who had managed to get a ticket. They had come to see their exiled prince return to the ring and begin his march to reclaim his throne.

Ali understood the importance of the fight to black Americans and to blacks around the world. There was great pressure on him to win. "I'm not just fighting one man," he said before the bout. "I'm fighting a lot of men, showing them that here is one man they just couldn't conquer. Lose this one, and it won't be just a loss to me. So many millions of faces around the world will be sad; they'll feel like they've been defeated." But Ali had no intention of losing. In round three, one of his razor punches opened a ghastly cut over Jerry Quarry's eye. The fight was stopped, and Ali was declared the winner. Muhammad Ali was back.

Six weeks later, the National Association for the Advancement of Colored People (NAACP) went to court for Ali in New York. They convinced a judge to grant Ali permission to fight in New York State. On December 7, at Madison Square Garden, Ali battled a bruising Argentine fighter, Oscar Bonavena. It was a hard fight for Ali, but he finally knocked Bonavena out in the 15th. Ali now felt that he was back in fighting shape. It was time to reclaim his title. During his years of exile from the ring, various heavyweights had fought to claim Ali's vacant throne. The man who emerged with the title was Joe Frazier.

Joe Frazier had battled his way up from poverty in South Carolina to success as a prizefighter. Unlike Ali, there was nothing graceful about Frazier's boxing style. Frazier was a fighting machine. He was a compact package of muscle, power, and stamina. In the ring, he did not know how to back up. From the opening bell, he waged nonstop war on his opponents. He came forward like a huffing, puffing locomotive, which earned him his nickname—"Smokin' Joe." He had explosive power in both fists. His most fearsome weapon was his left hook—a truly frightening punch when Frazier threw it. His opponents claimed it whistled like a missile. Between fights, he trained like a maniac. Frazier was undefeated, with 24 knockouts in 26 fights.

Ali desperately wanted to fight Frazier. Frazier had his title. Frazier wanted to take on Ali just as badly. Frazier was officially the heavyweight champ. But he knew that he would never be recognized as the true champion until he beat Muhammad Ali. The public was clamoring to see the fight; two undefeated heavyweights, perhaps the best of their time, clashing head to head for the title. It did not take long for the battle to be arranged. Ali and Frazier signed a contract to fight on March 8, 1971, at Madison Square

Garden. Each fighter would receive $2.5 million, a huge sum in those days.

Never in the history of boxing has so much excitement been generated by a fight. There was feverish anticipation across the nation. Originally called "The Fight of the Century," it soon became known simply as "The Fight." On the night of the bout, there was an electric atmosphere inside the packed Madison Square Garden. The fighters were introduced. Frazier looked like a man with a job to do. Ali danced round the ring gaily. "This may shock and amaze ya," he had rhymed before the fight, "but I'm gonna retire Joe Frazier."

During the first rounds, Ali jabbed and moved. Frazier came forward, trying to get within punching distance. Ali attempted to punish Frazier's face as he came in. He talked to Frazier, taunting him. Many of Ali's punches missed. Ali was still rusty from his long layoff, and Frazier was hard to hit because he moved his head constantly as he advanced. But many of Ali's punches found their mark. During rounds four and five, the fight began to change. Frazier was walking right through Ali's punches. He launched a brutal attack on Ali's body. The assault continued through rounds six, seven, and eight. Frazier's body blows were tremendous. The entire crowd gasped in unison as they landed. Ali rallied in flurries, taking a toll on Frazier's face. But Frazier came on, driving Ali to the ropes and hammering his ribs.

By round nine, Frazier was doing the talking. He bullied Ali around the ring. His body attack had weakened Ali. Frazier began to land thudding blows to Ali's head. He would land a terrific left to Ali's ribs, causing Ali to bend forward. Then Frazier would explode a left to Ali's head. Ali fought back ferociously with vicious combinations to Frazier's face. Frazier waded through them. In round 11, Frazier crashed one of his left hooks to Ali's jaw. Ali wobbled across the ring like a drunken man. He survived the round on sheer courage. Ali fought desperately for the

*Joe Frazier's arm is raised in victory after his defeat of
Ali in their heavyweight championship bout at Madison
Square Garden in March 1971. Frazier and Ali would
meet again in the ring.*

next three rounds, inflicting still more damage on Frazier's face. But Frazier was relentless. In the last round, he flattened Muhammad Ali with one of his missiles, knocking his opponent on his back. Ali was up quickly, but he was a badly damaged fighter. He stayed on his feet until the final bell, but the victory was clearly Joe Frazier's.

Dr. Ferdie Pacheco (right) and Angelo Dundee (left, with towel) try to convince Ali to get off the ropes in between rounds of Ali's fight with George Foreman in Zaire, Africa, in 1974. But Ali had his own ideas about how to beat the powerful Foreman.

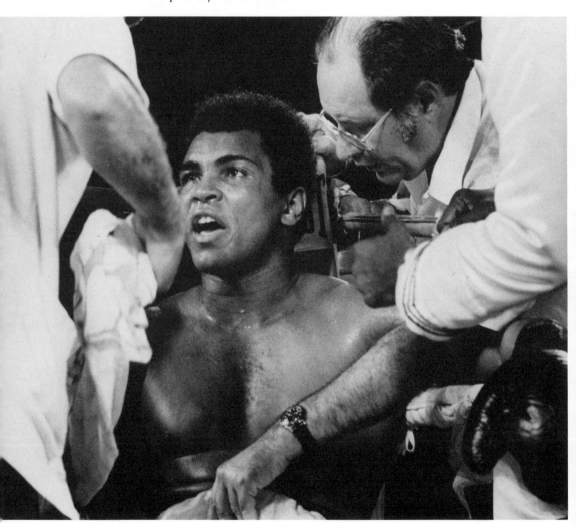

6

The Warrior

The loss to Frazier was devastating. But Ali responded with the heart of a warrior. He took six months off to recover from the brutal bout. During this period, Ali's conviction for draft evasion was reversed by the U.S. Supreme Court. Ali was once again a free American citizen. He could now fight whomever, whenever, and wherever he chose. So Ali fought everyone in sight. From 1971 to 1974, he took on what seemed to be the entire heavyweight division. He fought 13 times. He lost only one of these fights. The defeat came in March

1973 to a brawling former U.S. Marine, Ken Norton. Norton broke Ali's jaw in the first round. Despite the tremendous pain he was in, Ali finished the 12-round fight and almost won. Six months later he avenged the loss by whipping Norton, even though Ali broke his right hand early in the fight and was forced to battle Norton with one hand.

On January 28, 1974, Ali faced Joe Frazier again in Madison Square Garden. Smokin' Joe was no longer champion. He had lost the title a year earlier to a monster named George Foreman. It was an awesome display of punching power. The frightful Foreman had clubbed Frazier to the floor six times in the first two rounds to take the heavyweight title. The winner of the second Ali-Frazier bout would get a shot at Foreman and the crown.

The second Ali-Frazier contest belonged to Ali. It was a hard-fought 12-rounder. But Ali was stronger this time. Frazier had yet to recover from the savage pounding Foreman had given him. Ali outfought Frazier, wobbling him on several occasions. Ali still could not stop Smokin' Joe, who shook Ali at times and battled to the final bell. But the victory was undoubtedly Ali's. And the fight was barely over before Ali started talking about George Foreman.

It was called the "Rumble in the Jungle"— Muhammad Ali against the champion, George Foreman. The "rumble" took place before 64,000 chanting Africans in the steaming heat of Zaire, Africa, on the night of October 29, 1974. Nobody thought Ali had a chance. At the time, Foreman was much like Sonny Liston, except he was bigger, stronger, younger, he hit harder, and, if possible, he was meaner. He crushed opponents with his massive fists. Many experts considered him the most devastating puncher in heavyweight history. Ali, now 32 years old, was too old to handle him, everyone said. Foreman was too young, too strong, too powerful. Ali's only chance was to jab and run. But his aging legs would eventually give way, and Foreman would catch him. It would be a sad, and perhaps tragic, ending to a remarkable career.

Instead, the Rumble in the Jungle was Muhammad Ali's greatest moment as a ring strategist. To the shock of everyone, including Angelo Dundee, 64,000 Africans, announcers and writers from around the world, and most of all, George Foreman, Ali did not run. He lay on the ropes and let Foreman hit him! Big George obliged. He pounded away at Ali. At first, it seemed Ali was trapped on the ropes by Foreman's bulk. Dundee and Ali's helpers screamed at Ali to get off the ropes, to move and jab.

But as the fight continued, it became apparent that Ali had a plan. George threw his sledgehammer blows. Ali caught them on his gloves. Ali turned slightly to catch them on his shoulders, on his hips. He deflected them with his arms, leaned back at the last second as they hissed past his face. He smothered them, ducked them, rolled with them, used the ropes behind him as shock absorbers. He clinched with Foreman on the ropes and tied up his arms. He leaned on Foreman, resting his full weight on the big man's neck and shoulders to tire him. Foreman simply could not land a clean blow. Occasionally, Ali fired back a machine-gun flurry at Foreman to let him know he was not hurt. And he talked to Foreman constantly. "George, you big ape, you can't hurt me," Ali told him.

The men in Ali's corner now watched in silent amazement. Between rounds, Ali told them that this was his "rope-a-dope" strategy. It was risky, but it worked. Throwing his bombs all night in the sweltering heat and Ali's constant clinching had drained Foreman. Ali's chatter, and Foreman's inability to hurt Ali, had demoralized the slugger. Suddenly, in round eight, Ali exploded off the ropes. With three clean, crisp punches to the jaw, he cut the exhausted Foreman down. Big George toppled like a mighty tree in the jungle. The huge crowd was in a frenzy. Ali was a magician, a slayer of giants. And, miraculously, he was champion of the world again.

Later that night, a heavy tropical rainstorm broke. Ali and his trainers drove down a jungle road to get to their camp. "All through the jungle," remembers Ali's doctor Ferdie Pacheco, "people were lined up along the road with children in their arms, waiting for Ali in the pouring rain."

After Zaire, the warrior fought on. Ali encountered his old archenemy, Joe Frazier, one more time, on October 1, 1975. Their third meeting, staged in Manila, the Philippines, was one of the greatest battles ever fought inside a boxing ring. Over 700,000,000 people watched it in 68 countries on closed-circuit television. Before the fight, Ali jokingly called the fight the "Thrilla in Manila." After the fight, Ali said it was "the closest to death" he had ever come.

The third Ali-Frazier match was a savage, toe-to-toe war. It raged for 14 rounds. The fighters inflicted terrible damage on one another. The battle came to a merciful end after the 14th round. Frazier's eyes were swollen shut, and his face was unrecognizable. Nevertheless, he attempted to rise

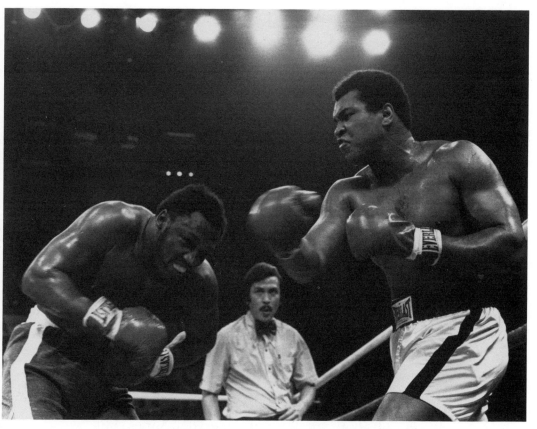

Ali hammers a right to the head of Joe Frazier as Frazier moves in low to unleash his body attack during the third fight between the two rivals. The grudge match, fought in Manila in October 1975, was a ferocious battle won by Ali when Frazier's trainer would not let his battered fighter come out for the final round.

from his stool for the final round. But his handlers would not let him. They held him on his stool and signaled the referee that their fighter was retiring. Ali was the winner, but he was too badly beaten to celebrate. He collapsed in a chair and held his head in his gloves. "He's the toughest man in the world," Ali said of Frazier shortly after the fight. "Man," Frazier said, "I hit him with punches that would bring down the walls of a city. Lawdy, Lawdy, he's a great champion."

Dr. Pacheco first advised Ali to retire after the third Frazier fight. "That's when he started to really fall apart," Pacheco said. A physical examination revealed that the champ's kidney's were badly damaged. He was displaying other alarming symptoms as well. Ali's speech was slightly slurred. His concentration wandered at times. His reflexes were slow. Ali was beginning to show the signs of 15 years of professional ring wars.

And what reason did he have to continue? He was now the most famous and beloved sporting figure in the world. He was entertained by kings and presidents in nations around the globe. Any lingering anger toward him in the United States had vanished after the Zaire miracle and his courageous third fight with Frazier. He was now regarded as a national treasure. He was invited to the White House for dinner. His appearance in public immediately drew huge, adoring crowds, both white and black. He had earned millions more than any fighter or athlete ever before. He had a beautiful, loving wife Veronica (his third), and many children. And he had the title. Why not retire now, at the peak of his fame and success?

But asking Muhammad Ali to walk away from the ring was like asking a painter to lay down his brush forever, or a writer to put down his pen and never write again. He continued to fight. But this was clearly not the same Ali. He lost his title to Leon Spinks in February 1978. In a final display of ring magic, he won it back six months later, becoming the first heavyweight to regain the crown three times. Now, surely, he would hang up the gloves and retire as champion.

But Ali fought again, and then again. In October 1980, Muhammad Ali lost his heavyweight title for the final time to Larry Holmes. Holmes was a young, skilled, hungry fighter. Ali had nothing left and was obviously a sick man. Holmes claimed that Ali was his idol and that he "loved" Ali. Nevertheless, he beat Ali terribly until the fight was stopped in the 10th round. Ali, incredibly, fought once more, in December 1981, losing in 10 rounds to Trevor Berbick in the Bahamas. He announced his retirement soon after.

Ali's physical condition continued to worsen. In 1984, he was diagnosed as suffering from Parkinson's syndrome. Parkinson's syndrome is a *neurological* disorder. In Ali's case, it was caused by the many head blows he received in the later stages of his career. Although the ailment causes such symptoms as difficulty in speaking, trembling of the hands, and slowness of movement, its progress can be halted with medication.

Because of his medical condition, many people now see Ali as a tragic figure. They believe he lives the life of an isolated cripple who spends his days lost in memories of a glorious past. This is far from the truth. Ali receives the best treatment available for his condition, which is stable. He lives on a farm in Michigan with his fourth wife, Lonnie Ali. He studies and practices Islam daily and entertains scores of visitors daily as well. When he is not at the farm, he is visiting sick children in hospitals or traveling around the world, usually to Third World nations, on missions of mercy. In 1990, he traveled to Iraq during the Gulf War crisis and met with Iraqi dictator Saddam Hussein. Ali spoke with Hussein and attempted to halt the oncoming war with the United States and its allies. When he returned home, Ali had with him 13 of the American hostages held by the Iraqis.

Ali entertains a crowd of admirers in China during one of his many trips to foreign countries. Since his retirement from boxing, Ali has not let anything—including illness—prevent him from spreading a message of hope and peace to peoples around the world.

Ali himself certainly does not feel tragic. "I had a good life before and I'm having a good life now," he said in 1991. "It would be bad if I had a disease that was contagious. Then I couldn't play with children and hug people all over the world. My problem with speaking bothers other people more than it bothers me. It doesn't stop me from doing what I want to do and being what I want to be. And now my life is really starting. Fighting injustice, fighting racism, fighting poverty, using this face the world knows so well, and going out and fighting for truth." Despite what many people think, Muhammad Ali's career as a fighter is not over. But now the whole world is his ring.

Further Reading

Buchard, Marshall. *Sports Hero: Muhammad Ali*.
New York: Putnam, 1975.

Denenberg, Barry. *The Story of Muhammad Ali,
Heavyweight Champion of the World*. New York:
Dell, 1990.

Edwards, Audrey. *The Picture Life of Muhammad Ali*.
New York: Franklin Watts, 1976.

Rudeen, Kenneth. *Muhammad Ali*. New York:
Crowell, 1976.

Schmity, Dorothy Childers. *Muhammad Ali: The
Greatest*. Mankato, MN: Crestwood House, 1977.

Wilson, Beth. *Muhammad Ali*. New York: Putnam, 1974.

Chronology

Jan. 18, 1942   Born Cassius Clay, Jr., in Louisville, Kentucky

1956–1960   Wins a succession of amateur titles

1960   Wins Olympic gold medal as light-heavyweight; professional boxing career begins

1964–1965   Defeats Sonny Liston in six rounds to become heavyweight champion of the world; announces his conversion to Islam and changes his name to Muhammad Ali; knocks out Liston in first round of rematch

1967   Ali refuses to be inducted into the armed forces; is convicted of draft evasion; boxing license is revoked in all states, and he is stripped of heavyweight title

1970   Acquires license to fight in Atlanta; stops Jerry Quarry in three rounds

1971	Ali beaten by Joe Frazier in 15 rounds for first professional loss; conviction for draft evasion overturned
1974–75	Outpoints Frazier in 12 rounds; knocks out George Foreman in eight rounds to regain heavyweight title; stops Frazier in 14 rounds
1978	Ali loses heavyweight title to Leon Spinks in 15 rounds; defeats Spinks in 15-round rematch to reclaim heavyweight title for the third time
1980–81	Ali loses to Larry Holmes in 11 rounds; loses to Trevor Berbick in 10 rounds; retires from boxing
1984	Diagnosed as suffering from Parkinson's syndrome
1990	Travels to Iraq to meet with Saddam Hussein in an attempt to ease tensions between Iraq and the United States; returns with 13 American hostages
1996	Ignites the Olympic torch at the Summer Games in Atlanta; receives honorary gold medal

Glossary

bout   a contest between two boxers

charisma   a magnetic charm or appeal inspiring personal loyalty or admiration

civil rights movement   the collective struggle to end racial discrimination and to gain equal rights for minorities

communist   a person who supports a social system, known as communism, in which there is in theory no private property or business and in which goods are owned in common and are available to all as needed

drafted   to be selected by the government for mandatory military service

extremists   those whose political or religious views or opinions are considered threatening by the majority of a society

76

fundamentals   the basic elements of a certain activity or practice

minorities   those members of a society who are different from others in some way and are often mistreated or looked down upon

neurological   having to do with the nervous system

persecution   the continual mistreatment of a person or a group, often for racial or religious reasons

segregation   the separation of members of a certain group or race from another group or race

spar   to box for practice, training, and conditioning

strategy   a careful plan or method

Index

Norman Macht holds a bachelor of philosophy degree from the University of Chicago and a master's degree in political science from Sonoma State University. He writes extensively on finance and sports history and has written several biographies for the Chelsea House BASEBALL LEGENDS series. Macht is also the author of *Christopher Columbus* and *Sojourner Truth* in the Chelsea House JUNIOR WORLD BIOGRAPHIES series.